DIASPORIC
VIETNAMESE
ARTISTS
NETWORK

DVAN Founders
ISABELLE THUY PELAUD
and
VIET THANH NGUYEN

Also in the series:

Constellations of Eve
Abbigail Nguyen Rosewood

Hà Nội at Midnight: Stories
Bảo Ninh; translated and edited by Quan Manh Ha and Cab Tran

Watermark: Vietnamese American Poetry and Prose, 25th Anniversary Edition
Edited by Barbara Tran, Monique Truong, and Khoi Luu

NOTHING FOLLOWS

POEMS BY

LAN P. DUONG

To Nataly, for living during the wake of war

Lan Duong 5/2023

TEXAS TECH UNIVERSITY PRESS

Designed by Hannah Gaskamp
Cover art *Between Home and Here 2* by Ann Le
Cover designed by spoon+fork

This book is typeset in EB Garamond. The paper used in this book meets the minimum requirements of ANSI/NISO Z39.48-1992 (R1997). ♾

Library of Congress Cataloging-in-Publication Data

Names: Duong, Lan P., 1972– author. Title: Nothing Follows / Lan P. Duong.
Description: Lubbock, Texas: Texas Tech University Press, [2023] |
Series: DVAN (Diasporic Vietnamese Artists Network) | Summary: "Memoiric poetry documenting a Vietnamese family's arrival in America"—Provided by publisher.
Identifiers: LCCN 2022060291 |
ISBN 978-1-68283-182-3 (cloth) | ISBN 978-1-68283-184-7 (paperback)
Subjects: LCGFT: Poetry.
Classification: LCC PS3604.U645 N68 2023 | DDC 811/.6—dc23/eng/20230208
LC record available at https://lccn.loc.gov/2022060291

Printed in the United States of America
23 24 25 26 27 28 29 30 31 / 9 8 7 6 5 4 3 2 1

Texas Tech University Press
Box 41037
Lubbock, Texas 79409-1037 USA
800.832.4042
ttup@ttu.edu
www.ttupress.org

for má
for ba

Contents

PART 3: THE LEAVING

Acknowledgments

There are many people who have helped me along this path—not the least my sisters, who have fed me stories from the beginning. I remember long ago, one sister wrote a short poem about orange peels when we arrived in Butler, Pennsylvania, a first encounter with the power of words that has followed me here. To my brother who, in his wayward ways, has inspired me to make art. And, of course, to my father and my mother whose devastating, complex lives constitute much of the book's stories.

I am also grateful for my friends from San José with whom I have shared the most beautiful and brutal memories together. They have lived in the lining of this book from its inception.

I am indebted to DVAN (Diasporic Vietnamese Artists Network) for providing me an opportunity to be at She Who Has No Master(s) retreats in Corsica and Djerassi, where I was nourished in ways that I never thought were possible. To Dao Strom for providing me guidance in the book's making. To Bao Phi and Mai Der Vang who gave me advice early on and whose own words inspired me to continue writing.

My most profound thanks to Isabelle Thuy Pelaud for supporting the collection even when I didn't have the strength to believe in it and for introducing my manuscript to Texas Tech University Press (TTUP). To Travis Snyder of TTUP for making this manuscript, after twenty-five years of my writing and rewriting it, into this material thing.

I want to thank the editors of the anthologies *Watermark* and *Tilting the Continent* for having published earlier versions of "Sister Play" as well as "The Healing" and "My Mother is Bụi Đời," respectively. The poetry journals *Spoon River Review* and *Oberon* also printed earlier versions of "In This House" and "Dragon."

And finally, my love to my greatest loves—Việt, Ellison, and Simone.

NOTHING FOLLOWS

PART ONE

THE FATHER'S HOUSE

San José, 1980

longhaired
dusty
bellbottomed,

emerging like wild things
from our wagon

and once again

we are

what we carry

clothes, pans
secondhand sandals

in our fists are rosaries
& several scapulars
each

a wooden clock
in the shape of Việt Nam
is what
Father brings
into the new house
two battered hands on

North and South

We left Butler

government cheese
a black clapboard house
railroad tracks

white Catholics
sponsoring us
from Việt Nam
to Guam

some of them
calling us gooks

no wonder
we are
here.

no wonder
we, sisters,
speak of
suicide
and other
dirty stories

no wonder
Father cannot

loses

his bearings
his temper
his tongue.

At 6
I am all eyes
full of
spit & spite

I am here
and it's a wonder
just

to begin
again.

Chapel Hill Way

The new house

is trimmed in shitbrown,

two   palm   trees

crouch dumbly

in the front yard

and because

Father has planted

a bomb

inside me,

at first blush, I cannonball
into the still dark

diving headfirst into mauve carpet

my brother tailing me

we are

spilling into
laughter,

fleeing doubles
for the other,

the same deeply-lashed eyes
our faces cracking open

like walnuts
when we try to smile

our bangs

    run across our foreheads

        like bandits in an open field

      the neighbors are truly. Alarmed.

white clouds of hair

    peeking

      behind lace curtains

      I pay them

no mind. Laughing ferociously,

      hands akimbo.   I am a cao bòi

and this here

      will be my wild west.

In This House

We take refuge from the wars
we had just come from and the wars
that were just beginning.
Father, who has carried all his battles
in his hands,
tattoos his rage onto our flesh,
one and one and one.

He was a lieutenant colonel
in the South Vietnamese army
and has lived through the French,
the Japanese,
and then, the Americans.
Wars he has known
he carefully places in the closet
a thick, triangular meat of a flag,
the three red stripes folded
onto yellow.

In this house we live
without the Mother
for far too long.
She will come later to America
to reunite with her children 20 years
after they left in 1975.
This armchair of a woman,
she does not tell us why
she stayed, cannot
for the life of her
tell us what she did
with the money.

In this house sisters' furies
are born. The anger of ớt
blooming on their skin like watercolors
(blues and purples mostly).
In this house the eldest brother
hatches a plan
to take his country back

from the communists.
In this house the artist brother
becomes a thief first,
and then, a runaway second.

In this house I always sleep
with 2 sisters
on a double bed.
In this house I grow an ache
for the snaking of
my arms with other arms,
the muscling of my legs
with their legs.

In this house I cut
fish with hands
that are really
like broken scissors in the kitchen.
I pull white hair
from black heads,
laying the threads on dark
in exquisite reticulate patterns.

In this house I use dầu xanh
on legs and temples,
nest fists into flesh,
and on summer nights, I skim
my sisters' backs as if
I was reading braille,
unseeding pustules of acne,
hard and small like grains of rice.

In this house my fingers absorb
all of the family's sicknesses,
their sweat and smell.
This is how I know they are family,
this is how I know they are mine.
Not by numbers
or other polite designations, but
the shape of their bodies,
the size of their pores.

In this house I devour my sisters'
fears and strengths—
every last one of them.
And on days they don't want to work,
I hold them still
and listen
(ear to belly)
to the eerie sounds of thunder
their stomachs make.

In this house I find the best hiding places
to fold my body into two
when the fighting becomes too intense.
In this house I touch
the nub of skin between my legs and
love myself open
during late summer evenings.

In this house I listen to stories
and scavenge for what is useful.
I take the fragments with me
for when I leave
and come back,
for when I leave
and come back.

CLOUD   ANCHOR   HOUSE

His hands are like the rough gloves
he uses for weeding.
They take mine
and we surface
from the Oldsmobile,
a yellow boat that
we sailed on from
Pennsylvania to California in 1979

We are an awkward couple,
a father, a daughter,
quiet we round the corners,
up the library stairs.
A chessboard is packed
tight under one
of his flanneled arms
and a goodwill
bag of books
hangs from the other

At the library he beats
men in chess.
They are Black Latino Chinese
old, some of them young,
some bearded, and most are ugly
murmuring, they eye
the daughter's thick calves
when she tiptoes and whispers
into the father's ear
is it time to go home yet?
and then they hit
their chessboards
with a loud

      THWACK!

At the library
I read to master the words of a language
he can barely speak. Because

he is the one who teaches me
how to read and spell first, swirling
letters in the air with one finger

CLOUD   ANCHOR   HOUSE

At the library,
I read all the dirty parts
in adult fiction
I scrawl the words fuck you
to those motherfuckers
who write on the bathroom walls
that nips are taking over San José.

I take the time to write
a letter to the staff saying:
To celebrate
Martin Luther King's birthday,
you've displayed all the flags
of the world,
but not my father's—
it's the one with 3
red stripes on yellow

At the library
I cut out pictures of
old Hollywood, with their strong
jawlines, straight noses, the kind of
max-factored beauty
I didn't know
Hedy Lamarr, Carole Lombard, (and later,
Marilyn Monroe),
replacing the photos
that pinned us in the local newspaper
where we're surrounded
by white sponsors, a whole congregation,
we are furtive, expectant,
the lines among us
indistinct.

At the library
I make my way

to the right angles of corners
and ride the sweep and bend
of English, using the words to
stitch for myself   a
grammar that makes sense
of the wilderness
of the war

and eventually,
I become what I know—a writer
who will tell dirty stories
about being a refugee,
about being a refugee girl,
about growing up poor in San José,
about counting those
who have come into my life
(because of the war) and
counting those who have left
(because of the war).

And when I stop
going to the library,
when I am no longer his girl,
and the prick of his hopes
pinned on me
no longer bleeds,
he will say to me,

"Your poems hurt me. I don't understand
what they mean. But I can tell you,
they are lies, and those lies
you've spread—they will shame me
long after I am gone."

Dragon

I crack bones
with the soles of my feet.
Sideways! Never vertical!,
my father grunts
when I walk on his back.
It is as straight, smooth and stiff
as a gangplank.

He lies prone
on our thickly corded mat,
his head lying next
to the threaded picture
of a dragon.
His hands lay at his side, open.

For a short time, his hands will not
be balled, gripping
a Chinese checker piece, or
wrapped around meat,
muscle or bone.

They remind me
of his hands in church
they sleep
while the black-frocked figure
at the pulpit
waves his own pink hands
wildly.

At 7, I know
this is good.
I don't have to look
at the whites of his eyes
the color of soiled sheets

Black head

Yellow back

Blue-striped pajamas

I walk on his back, cautious,
fearing the breaking of bones.
too early, too soon.
I am 45 pounds,
the youngest of his nine,
and I listen for the sharp blows
of his breath.

Right
at the point
where my feet are balanced
on the tightrope
of his narrow shoulders,

I step off.

I look at his chest,
the raised skin is
pink and puffy.
The intricate patterns
of the sinewy mat
are imprinted
on my father's chest.
It is the body of a fierce dragon.
And each time, I am in wonder
that I did that.

I did that.

Anything Almost Dead

In the summer

we are baked clay

in the house

but he

he is outside, burning

trash & dung

scorching the earth
&
pouring rat poison
into gopher holes
up to their necks

I see him, low
on his haunches,
scything

whole stalks of plants—
never mind that

they are still
growing—grasping
with military fists

He looks at me,

nods in the direction

of the terrified
weeds, and
says, no good.

&
with one finger,

he flicks his lighter,

a silver box
of flame that hisses
without its liquid,

incinerates
broken twigs
paper
cardboard—

anything almost dead,
he says

orange flames
& curling fumes
dance around him,

he looks like a mirage

my father
is a
lovely
beautiful
mirage.

Celebration

"I carried her in my arms when she was two years old, from Saigon to America. She was the one I carried—only her." I hear this story at every Celebration.

He finishes with a big smile; the one he reserves for people he hasn't met yet. And he goes out back, twists the head of a duck, and carves its feathered neck. He drains the blood into a tin pan; the red syrup we eat with peanuts browned over a stove.

He is chastised in the checkout line because we have more than 10 items. When the manager comes, the one with the face of a cauliflower plant, she tells us to get to the back of the line. My father's tongue half-nelsons some words but he can't pin anything down.

In other places, in other times, he speaks to me in Spanish, Latin, and French, beginning sentences with *moi*, and declaring, *la simplicité est la première beauté*. He tells me, chopsticks mid-air, "Did you know, fratricide comes from brother and -cide from killing. What about regicide?" At night, calling himself *señor* and me *señorita*, his hands double-jointed, contorted, his fingers are cocked, forming a rabbit, a dog, a man with a stovepipe hat.

He tells me he has gone from high school to seminary, joins the army, becomes an officer for the French and the Americans, fighting with his oldest son against the Việt Cộng. A father at 19, he arrives in the US with 7 children finds 3 houses to live in and eats welfare for 45 years. He tells me, "When the Japanese were in our country, they used our rice for fuel."

Trained at Fort Benning, he was an elite officer in a segregated South. He came back to his country a new man, he says. We leave Lion Supermarket. Collapsing into the car, he talks to himself, mucous gathering at both ends of his lips. I don't hear what he is saying.

The bottled juice breaks open, gurgling its sweet liquid, it pisses all over the back seat.

1985

arriving at SFO,
her cheeks in flames
by the Việt Nam sun.

kinky hair
orangered because of the perm
she got in the camps.

this sister
was left behind when we came
in '75.

She tended pigs on a farm
keeping secret his military history and
burying family   photos at   night

I watch her,
this woman parading
as my father's daughter.

squatting in the tub
feet apart,
calves bulging

her body

a terrain thick
with inflammation, swells of fat
deep necklaces of skin

in time
she feeds me stories,
and I devour them.

like when
she says Má married at 18
beaten by Ba by 19,

or that Má had 12 children (3 of them she buried)
because god-said-so and because our-uncles-who-are-priests
ordained it.

She tells me
in the language
of our familiar

about the uncle
in New Orleans,
who wears 3-inch heels

and beats
his wife with
a 12-inch stick,

and how all of our aunts and their children and their children's children
treated her no better than a dog
because she was left behind

California, Boston, and Back Again

she gets a job at an assembly plant
processing tomatoes,
vomiting on the way home,
she calls in sick
her body wants to quit

when no one's home
we walk to the video store
and check out porn with her alien card,
the one that has her left ear displayed
like a hibiscus
pinned to the head

the video clerk doesn't say anything
the form he makes us
fill out every *single* time
requires a phone number,
and so, to the black pen
he grips in his hand,
I whisper, bốn không tám,
hai chín hai, bảy bảy ba năm

the VHS is placed in a clean
black bag, we insert it
into a black box
at home and then
we're laughing actually
our thick pale legs stacked
like lunch meat on the couch

at 30, she moves
to Boston with a boyfriend
to get out from father's grip
anh Hải is bespectacled,
slight, bookish, and horny,
she tells me, with a crooked finger.

returning to California
much later
she sees
she does not fit
into the folds of our family.

We are
a frayed piece of cloth,
with no ends and corners
she can meet
with her own.

the time apart
between us
too hard, and
we're talking
in her foil-lined kitchen
in her 2bd rental
on King Road

where the persimmons are orange fists
on a platter
our legs crossed underneath the table,
not reaching the linoleum floor,
they're swinging heavy

she is preparing her only son's meal
cá kho tộ canh chua đậu hũ nhồi thịt

Hotel California

The scars on his back
are medallions
he never received
for fighting the
Việt Cộng in 1972,
they lay on the surface
of his skin
that is mottled, dusted
with ash—all this
is good camouflage
in the jungle,
he tells me.

But here,
under the California sun,
they've turned yellow,
the color of cork.
They are round
watermarks
he cannot blot,
pocked landmarks
he cannot
return to.

In time, he works
part-time,
full-time,
over-time,
all-the-time
for a tech company
in Sunnyvale.

Bringing his work home,
he's a card dealer,
laying out the raised, pimply
motherboards,
his back arched
over sharp pins
until early morning.

Tuesdays, his lank body is
planted in front of the TV,
smoking Marlboro Reds,
he's laughing at Jack
from Three's Company.
One hand is snaked
underneath his shirt, and
I catch him fingering
all the places
he's been.

Fridays, he's shooting
bi da at Club Eden
his body slouched
felt green, a long-nailed finger
curved around a stick—
the eye of a needle

Other times,
he's just gone.

And that's when
my sisters and I huddle,
talking and shucking
seeds with teeth
and tongue.

And we go,

He went where?/No, I haven't talked to him/No, I haven't seen him/Yes, I'll call around,
try to find him/ I won't tell Ba/He told me he was going back to Việt Nam, couldn't live here
anymore, he wanted to kill all the communists/He shaved his head again/Doesn't he know,
doesn't he understand?/He just can't do this kind of thing here/The last time I talked to him,
he was kinda drunk, kinda high/He said, em, my country is breaking my heart.

Sister Play

Because there weren't
enough beds,
I sleep with my sisters.
Our legs would lock
together
at night.
Our legs, which were
like the pliers
father used
to play
the handyman,

were hard
and muscular, because
we took after
our stout mother,
our sturdy calves
reminding us of
where we come from,
that we inherited
more than just
pimply backs and
an ironic fear of men,
but that we could endure
and endure
for a long time
after that,
too.

It's like
this one time,
we're at the playground,
and everything around
us is FIRE!

I am holding on
because she's 4 years older,
gripping my legs
with fingertips

not yet painted
with the brush
of puberty.

We're struggling
against the smooth evil
of the aluminum,
our sweet girlsweat
only making the slide slicker,
we hold on because
we have to,
TAKE MY HAND!,
then cawing with laughter.

We play until
the slide becomes
cool and indifferent
to our skin,
and we leave
with the brown of bark on
our elbows.

We sleep well
these nights,
fingers laced,
our strong legs hurting
a little from our play,
muscle
the other, and
we lay
stronger
than rope, cord, or twine.

Roman Holiday

My god, she is beautiful.

Dark brown eyes, slim calves,
and a lovely nonchalance

I only hoped
to acquire
someday.

Because Má was being held hostage
by COMMUNISM in Việt Nam,
she took my hand and

we danced the Tango, the Cha-Cha,
the Be-bop and the Boston;

the main ingredients of
any kind of social life,
she says.

She tells me about
father's ugly childhood,
his beatings, *his* inability to father

us properly
and how the key

to anything
really
was acceptance.

She says, never give in to a guy;
he'll disrespect you in so many ways.

One guy, though, blows
her   mind
and leaves

the remains in the

middle of the bed
rotting
like wild cabbage.

"Poor child," my aunt says,
turning rosary beads
in one hand

She's just flown in from Texas
when she hears
about her catatonia.

thằng khốn nạn,
she says,
in vulgar Vietnamese

I spit out, You're wrong!

Just the other night, she came in and told me there was an Audrey Hepburn movie on. It's the one where she's this beautiful princess in Italy and she runs away, falls in love with the wrong guy, this news reporter—I forget the name of the movie but in the end, she's had fun, and she has to go back to being a princess . . . remember?

Yeah, and when it was over, we held each other and cried.

Yeah, that's the one.

The Healing

she is sick
of caring
for the sick
she falls
on the bed,
the dress patterns
crackling

fire underneath her body
that will later shelter
spools of cancer
daisy chained
across her chest, but

at 8, I am not
afraid of this. Yet.
I cạo gió for her
the best I know how

I straddle her waist
my strong legs looking inert
next to hers,
because she is strong and
we are strong
inheriting
our limbs from Má

I eye her open back
the pustules of acne
are fleshy studs
fastened into a wall

Because Má ate too much ớt,
it's in our blood,
she lets me know.

I rain eucalyptus oil
in burning green puddles
in the trenches of her back

that has bowed
to the elders of ours,
to the father, the brother
and the son,

I scrape her back
with the edges of a quarter,
past the scars and
ridges of spine,

hard and harder still—until
spittles of blood

       break
the surface of skin.

until the bruising
takes the shape of
ribs,
a striking
column of bone.

then
when   the blood is   released,
she draws this deep breath
and sleeps,

and all the while
the cool green
rides
in my hair

for days.

The Mosquitoes in Guam

God, it's always
with that
muffled voice
of his like—
he's been bagged

and taken hostage
the words   escaping
from one
side of his mouth
Houdini-like.

My brother the artist asks,

"Do you know what happened in Guam?"

We're driving to get some beer
he's 15, I'm 9,
cruising in the Chevy
Chevette on Story Rd
the 8-track
wailing REO Speedwagon.

And he begins like this

we were in the camps, and
it was late
Ba's sleeping 3
cots away,
his mouth an O
mosquitoes buzzing
under the fluorescents

hissing

a guy sits next to me, shifts
the green blanket away, asking me
if I'm okay
why can't I sleep, the mosquitoes, I tell him, & the heat
     he smiles

and puts one hand

up my shirt in my shorts—
crawling like soldiers on a battlefield.

the other covers my mouth
     smelling like eggs and gasoline

My brother the artist says this all
in one big paragraph—
like he's been rehearsing
for a long time now

My brother the artist
has been raised
by sisters who are
more like his brothers
all of us
too strong,
all of us—
loving—
too much, too soon—
already?
and now—
not enough.

That night, I play dead
and for many nights after that, too.
     Like a bear has clawed my throat

a column
of mangled
flesh

You should have seen by the look in my eyes, baby
there was somethin' missin'

you should have known by the tone of my voice, maybe
but you didn't listen

and I think about
how this one time
he came out of juvie
caught
              stealing a purple bike for me

he put together a shadowbox
cotton, glue, glitter, some twigs
and when he was done, I gasped

there was

a lone house
a wooden fence
a moon
two
three
wondrous hills.

PART TWO

ĐỦ MÁ SAN JOSÉ

At 9

I walk alone
                     to school
along the way
          men in their Pontiacs
                     jerk off after
the school bell rings

at RFK elementary
the boys
                 dry hump me
in the bathroom
                and some girl swings
an aluminum bat
                  at my knees
                       during PE

Mr. Wooley
              makes all the
                   Southeast Asian girls
      do push-ups
                      on black pavement,

his oblong face so close to our
                immigrant tits

in the class picture

I am in scarlet red
                    to the far left,
my hands to the side,
            balled,
my mouth
         a longragged gash
on a smooth face

I decide then
          that I must find friends

         feral like me.

Hiền

has 4 moles
on each side
of her face
brown hair shorn
best thing is,
she doesn't
give a rat's ass
about boys, or
the pretty Filipinas
and their hello kitty gear

red tracksuits
every day of the week,
she and her sisters
walk to school
from Santee Apts.
in 3s, taking up
the whole sidewalk

since they escaped
in '81 by boat,
they've always
dressed the same,
always been close.

Hiền does phim chưởng moves
on a boy named Bradley,
who calls her
bitch for no reason.
He backs off,
& we laugh straight
into his face.

in class she whispers
words like cu and chim
to me and shares
mechanical pencils she's lifted
we sign our names on books
wrapped in brown paper bags.

At the Indian-owned
liquor store, Imperial,
she swipes
boxes of lemon drops
now and laters
pop rocks.

She pours them
in my mouth
I'm blowing out dust
and fire

And when we leave,
the gummy worms,
their bodies,
dangle
from our pants pockets,
the sugar frosting
our fingertips

Barbie

on our bikes,

           our girlbodies   pitch   forward

                    like arrows on   bows

while the Barbies
in our hands
        are tightly fisted

              around chrome
                 that is freckled with rust

there is spit & laughter & wind

       when we round a corner

at the Santee Apts.

           3 boys jump us while 1

              goes straight

          for me, his skin the color
of nước mắm,
             an arm hooks my body
                like a fishing rod

his fingers cover one breast,

       lay horizontal against

             the stripes of
my sailor tee, & with

the other hand, a finger pokes inside
       and digs around.
             like a mechanic
underneath the hood
             of a car.

Hiền is on the shorn grass,

        her legs spread   wide   open
                boyhands
rubbing clumsy

                            on her crotch

her white vans are stained a

                  beautiful kelly green

finally

        a car comes through,

                and they run away

but even so,
        they're kicking stones

              fists raised

we mount our bikes then   taking time

            to avoid pitted streets

while our Barbies' eyes

are sparkling   pretty

Refugee Teeth

some days

we let our skin ripen
                                yellow to brown
and play jacks
    during the lightest
shade of evening,

with chopsticks
& tennis balls

we braid Chinese jump rope
with the toes of our feet and the gaps
            in   between.

and when we are done with that, too,
our legs stretch   out
                        small Vs
on each side of a board game,
buying hella properties
when we pass GO!.

some days
                we find 75 cents,
in the cleavages   of   couches,

dodging the cars
            on Tully
                        like Frogger.

we jump in
                        —hands clasped,
noses pinched—
                into the pool at McKinney

the seed of yellow
                        in my bathing suit
growing permanent those days

and then other days,
        I hear

                              Why's your friend so dark!

              sniggering

And then, *hahahaha*!

these words are power,   I know they hurt

they are as jagged as my
                refugee teeth

what I don't tell people is her lips
are wondrous
                        and that
when she and I grow up
        years after McKinney Pool
closes
              because of a shooting—
        blood seeping deep
into concrete veins

our secrets, our sex, will always be entwined
like licorice vines.

I know that

boys like those beautiful broad-faced twins
Hùng and Sỹ

are going to be hella crazy
for her lips,
on necks and dicks

they're the ones
                who tell me what I already know.

those lips are crazy
        good for hickeys

and long exquisite blows.

Fragmented Reason

When Ba finds work
as a printer's assistant,
he makes stacks
& stacks of business cards
for me.

I don't have a job.
I'm only 10.

The cards list
my name & address,
embossed on each
side is a thicket
of bông mai.

He gifts me
with his talent
he wanted to be
an artist but was
pushed into the military
and then
the seminary
by the hands and feet
of a grandfather
I never wanted to meet.

The artist in him
christens me
with a waterfall
of names in
iambic pentameter.

It begins first
with our surname,
followed by a word
that marks me as Girl, and then,
another—either
American, or Beautiful,
I think.

It ends with
a coupling
of smell & sound –
perfumed orchid

While others in my family
are Beautiful Tear,
Fragmented Reason,
and Fragrant Autumn,
I am his last,
his smallest,
the one born before
the war ends & the one
who'd leave
his country
with him

soon after
he is crushed
by the weight
of another flag

Brass in Pocket

I'm kicking it
        with my homegirls
eating now and laters

when I see her broad shoulders first
                the one on the swings

              who
I think I'm
                      supposed to fight—
Dog! Bitch! Let's go!
words poppin' out of my mouth
          like gunshots

she swings first,
fingers in my hair
                knees me   deep
in my stomach

kick her ass! kick her ass!
my friends yell

her hands hold my head
                    right above the concrete,
I imagine a strawberry stain   next

      to spilt ice cream and then   I'm screaming,

      I'm sorry! I'm sorry! I'm sorry!

she makes me say it

      over and over,
          so, I say it over and over.

then gives me one good shake
              like a dog after it pisses

      my face streaked

with dirt raw scratches,

Tiger, tiger burning bright!

brass in pocket
                    I walk home,

          alone   fingering the rings

this fight tells me
                    I can't fight for shit,

          and I have to be   the one to jump first.

First comes summer, then comes fall

I'm home late cuz

ms. Kulzer asked me to
wipe the chalkboard clean

when I hear people say

she was raped   he   her

a brown corduroy skirt
a silver watch

a family friend

      we don't know anything,

do you?

I go to her house every day,

I ask her pretty mom,
      and all of her

pretty sisters,
        they tell me she's too sick

to play, to go to the pool

      weeks after &

itscoldwetrainy

      I finally see her.
we're outside

    her house

      lily of the niles

ring her doorway

they are open-mouthed and   taut

I don't

      fold her
                  in my arms
like I want to. I'm afraid,

actually,

      that what happened to her
                  will happen to me,

      that I will catch it, and

I will be caged

      for a long time,

           an awful beast.

The Furies

I.   Before the acne pits

     my skin like bullet   holes

   across my face and back

         my father says
with terrific venom

   Don't eat all that ót!
        You're going to end up just like your mother, your sisters!

He leaves, and I just

   become extra discreet,

methodical even, in eating

the thing he hates

    so much.

I take out
      the baloney

the color of my nipples

I lay it on a slice of
    white bread, snowing its backsides

with black pepper.

I eat it in gulps one, two, and three
          and choke.

Gunpowder shoots down
   my-just-taken-out-tonsiled throat

      Father, take me to the hospital—please

II. But   wait

                wasn't she carted there,

packed like ice

                    by men in blue.

dragged

by his army-issued hands   across   wet   cement,

I had to call the police,
           right?

at the hospital
            the doctors blotted out
the poisons in her body,

      charcoal
            in her mouth,
a tongue
        mottled like mold.

my tonsils were taken out there

            while father held my hand,   and promised me

that I'd grow taller. a scoop of vanilla   ice cream

to make it better, he said.

III.   I remember   then
          where I am now
& I get some water
knock it back
like a shot

I feel better, a lot better.

and then I start to

I eat mad ót
                    like my mother and
all of my sisters.

ót is chili peppers,
chili powder
chili flakes

anything that makes me hiss with pain.

a ritual

of eating it

          when he isn't around,
                    and even later

                    when he is

     IV.   and eventually, because I eat

               so much of it,
                         the sores
          in my mouth are
                    whiteyellow islands

of infection, the edges of
               my tongue serrated
                    like a knife.

In time, I feel like with   everything
I've eaten, with everything

I've taken in,

               I have   finally

become my sisters'
          their furies, their madness.

and all I want to do is fuck things up.

I am a bright, red phosphorous tip

on a single match, ready to strike

        V.   later when I finally get

my period,

       and even as I   howl
               in the school bathroom
          because I want to stay 12 forever,   I am ready

             for the blood,

the wars, and the ravages
             that take over   my body

     soon after.

Hey Baby, what did you do to summer, and what did summer do to you?

When Mỹ asks her this,
he pushes his fake
ray bans
down his nose,
looks at her body
side to side,
up and down,
& around

when he asks her this,
he says something
I've always known—
that Trinh *is* summer,
with legs
smooth and thin
as freeway rails,
white straight teeth
that never needed
fixing

when he asks her this,
he's licking his lips,
the hair on his upper lip
twitching.

when he asks her this,
I know we've crossed
some line,
like we've made it
to some place
that we're not
coming back from

when he asks her this,
we're into this thing called
New Wave—
our hair feeling

like cotton candy,
our asses looking
like lollipops
in tight jeans

when he asks her this,
we're cutting school
almost every day,
smoking in 4s,
and hanging out
with the boys
from Oak Grove
even more.

when he asks her this,
our sex has been
holstered to our sides
& we are
cocked
and ready to go.

We Refugee

we refugee

                                we be running schemes

scoring money from men who just came

                   by   boat

without wives

                    kids

some of them

        reeducated

               most of them

                broke

we refugee

        we be hanging

                   at the pool hall

talking to chú Triết,

              who loops his belt twice

        he bends his car antenna

in the shape of a heart, asking me nice,

              em thích không?

we refugee

          we be folding napkins

              2 cents each

cutting peaches

        at the cannery

              off Meridian,

smelling like industry

          at least once a week

we refugee

          we be slamming waves

at the beaches

               fighting at the rink

                      saying *aaaayyyyy*, what's up?

two hands cupped in the air
                to all the fly guys
                                in their Cavariccis

we refugee

        we be straddling these here streets

        bụi đời cowboys

                on Capital & King

                        Senter & Story

listening to our own badass beats

Cutting

we think
we're so cool,
saying we birthed
coolness and shit—
like
Miles Davis
had nothing on us
and shit,
hangin'
with the ultra-fresh
Filipinas and Latinas
saying things like,
the higher the hair,
the higher the đủ má heel!
and shit
taking off
our hoops
when we
need to fight,
cutting classes
on the regular,
writing notes
to teachers
about taking off
three days for Tết
waiting for the boys
from Oak Grove
to pick us up
cuz they're our

homecheez

and we're their

homegurlz

in their tricked out cars

booming high energy

tee-peeing houses

of tị nạn families

being chased

by parents

in their flip flops

scratching the cars

of girls we don't like,

battling the ones

we wanna fight,

and listening close

to the mad cute boys

scratching vinyl

fighting on the streets

of San José,

jumping in

to help my homegirl

cuz she's being called a nip—

getting clocked

in the eye,

and it's puffy

like cooked shrimp

and then—

here I am

going to church

every Sunday,

memorizing scripture

in Vietnamese

and English
watching the green berets
sitting close to him,
resting hands near
his soccer-
scarred knees

The Edge

Giỏi
has a *sick*
ass car,
a beautiful teal
Honda Civic
with subwoofers
as big as
coffins.

We ride
with him
to The Edge
our fake IDs
get us in,
and then
drenched
in hip hop beats,
our sex as thick
as legs in denim shorts

the guys with
their rooster hair
leaning against the wall—
a quivering skyline
and then
we're trembling
to that deep bass
keep jinglin' baby

people call us
the Great Wall
of China, but we don't care
they don't fuck with us
and we don't
fuck with you

until someone
does and then, first,
it's the fists,

and second, the kicks.
then outside
for a smoke

Giỏi taps
a cigarette
with a long
fingernail,
lights it up,
passes it
around.

me, Hiền,
Trinh & Tâm
we're savoring
the click
the burn
of the thing,
the smoke
sucked deep
into our
young lungs.

under the lights
Giỏi's hair
hangs off
to the side
like a cliff,
keys
in one hand
jangling, sweating, mating

They say that
when his
homey died
off the 17,
Giỏi cried
like a bitch

But tonight,
he's calm,
he's *excellent*.

I'm eyeing
his car, high
from the smoke,
and I think
that hell yeah, the color
of cool is teal

then he asks, em đi chơi hông?

It's 1AM,
and even though
I know
Father will call me
a whore
and even though
I know
Giỏi has 5 Ts
tattooed
on his left hand
(for tình, tiền, tù, tội, thù),

I go.

Babyface

boys swaggering in at 2
in the morning
to Dennys
                tent-like
                        white tees,
flared blue jeans
sewn together
3 panels on each leg.
                  LA style, they said.

Babyface
slides in
He's 15

but he looks 11
a Vietnamese Opie
he introduces his homies
                  Johnnie, Sammy and TC (tay chơi)

Big Tony is the oldest,
his zitty face looking like
                  chunky soup.

Their crew steals cars,
                  leaving them behind on the 5.

Exchanging numbers
he beeps my friend
that same week.

4-3-4
let's meet at a motel
Les Amis
                  on First Street.

Paris by Night is on repeat
Babyface takes out a gun.
says they're gonna
                  rob a jewelry store on Tully

he lets me hold it
and I hold the glock
            a finger in its hole

and give it back, but not before
I grip it once,
            then twice more

He's saying he likes me, that
I look sweet
            and chucks my chin

We leave, and for a long time,
no beeps, no meets.

then he's on the news:

a Vietnamese gangster arrested for B&E
he got assault
with a deadly weapon.
                        15 years

Ritual

Father buys me
a car at auction
when I'm 15,
an '82 Honda

Accord hatchback,
two gunshots
on the side
He makes me

buy insurance.
He says,
"You must be careful—
always."

He places a picture of
Jesus Christ
on the dashboard
(the one where His heart

wears a crown of thorns).
He says,
"He will protect you."
Father changes

the oil every 3 months.
Clinging to the car's underside,
first his black head emerges,
then gangly body
in threadbare pajamas

He washes his hands
with Ajax,
the white powder eating
his skin.

He uses bleach to whiten
my scuffed sneakers
when I grow from 10 to 14

I say, "Father, thank you.
But your hands—"

soon though
I grow eyes and ears
and my heart breaks
with the kind of grief
that his hands have
grown seeded & sown

I am full now
of stories of joy
and terror
that I need to tell.

I let the insurance lapse,
Jesus's picture is scratched off,
the halo around him a fatty yellow

and I turn to the church
of the streets

I say to him, "the engine keeps
choking and it stalls
when I need
to keep going."
He doesn't answer.

Sitting on his couch,
a red velvet blanket
engulfing him in fire,
he strums his guitar and sings
about returning
to Việt Nam
one day.

3x

1. He drives on St. James Street. Encapsulated in his shit-brown, '85 Toyota Corolla, he doesn't recognize me, doesn't hear the loud honking. At 68, his hands grip the wheel, he is terrified of looking to the left or right, just straight ahead.

2. He boils rau muống for me when I am home, every now and then. The slender tendrils of drab green, once the color of his fatigues, lie on a plastic Chinese plate. A small bowl of nước chấm, swirling with garlic, is placed nearby. Like the monk that he was supposed to become, my father has never put enough ớt in the sauce, not allowing the bite of the chili's sting on his tongue.

3. Ba? I call out. I find him on the double bed, his bulbous veins are the noodles we used to eat on Sunday mornings. They are roped around his hands. He is humming Ave Maria. In a voice mauled by all the Marlboros he's smoked, he tells me he has cried for me on 3 occasions in our lovely, but brutal, life together.

1: when we are picked up at shore
2: when he finds an American hospital in Guam because I am running a high fever
3: when I go to preschool for the first time, and the nuns of Butler usher me in.

I am smiling, he says, when I leave him behind.

PART THREE

THE LEAVING

Sweet Shrimp the Color of Oranges

When Má arrives at the airport, she's holding a clear plastic bag marked "IOM," where
her paperwork has lived for the past 20 years. Persephone leaving another world.
In my hands are two balloons.

Wearing her best aó dài, her feet are shod in ornate slippers that have permanently
deformed her feet; her toes are fanned to the right and left like the grooves on a seashell.
For today she has painted her toenails red, and they look like fallen pomegranate seeds.

She smells like what I will later know to be Đồng Nai, of charcoal bits, red earth, a
pig farm nearby. She smiles, and her teeth are lovely, broken and brown. Her nose a
clove of ginger squatting in the middle of her small face, and eyes bruised a light brown.

She sees me, but doesn't recognize the daughter she has not seen in twenty years,
doesn't recognize the body she's bequeathed me, strong limbs, a muscular frame.
Her arms tight around me, she speaks into my pockmarked cheeks.

And then, at the house, after all the well-wishers are gone, the guava cake eaten, and
red-wrapped gifts lay on the floor splayed open: dried, sweet shrimp the color of
oranges, cuttlefish powdered with dust and white, my mother takes a bath.

Her gambler's laugh is thick when she undresses, her hips a large sink and breasts
that reach deep into the water. I watch her when eldest sister washes her, a hand towel
with green soap.

My Mother is Bụi Đời

Her brown-sweatered torso
lies in front of me
on the single bed
she has claimed hers
for the next three months.

My mother is bụi đời,
she likes to leave
đi lang thang,
my sisters tell me.

I bunch the thick knit of
sweater up and around her neck.
Her skin has collapsed
like heavy socks.
Her back as wide and clean
as a cutting board.

My sisters tell me that the pustules
of acne are strands of pearls
she has lovingly
passed down to us

They tell me we're heirs
to her generosity
when she wandered
around villages, gambled, burned
money without prayers,
on solid legs that
did not lend her any roots.
My mother is bụi đời.

Now, pushing the ache
from her body,
I see her back,
it only shows traces of fight,
the anger of ớt
faint bird tracks
on a barren road.

This Is What I've Been Told

She stayed behind in Việt Nam because she didn't want to be a part of his life.
She stayed behind in Việt Nam because she didn't want to be a part of our lives.
She stayed behind in Việt Nam because she wanted her own life.
She stayed behind in Việt Nam because she wanted to make her own choices.
She stayed behind in Việt Nam because she felt like she had no other choice.
She stayed behind in Việt Nam because she wanted to.
She stayed behind in Việt Nam because she had already left the children behind, why not another time?
She stayed behind in Việt Nam because she had to pay back debts.
She stayed behind because she was beaten and didn't want to stay with him.
She stayed behind in Việt Nam because she thought it would get better.
She stayed behind in Việt Nam because she didn't want to mother.
She stayed behind in Việt Nam because she wanted to leave the father.
She stayed behind in Việt Nam because she couldn't imagine a life outside of Việt Nam.

What We Say When We Talk about Việt Nam

I.

Did you hear?
Trí, our cousin, the son of bác Lưu, hanged himself?
No, I didn't know. What happened? We are not sure, he was only 16 but he hated being under his mother's thumb, all the time, he was.
I saw him in 2005, he said hello from a corner of the room, a white shirt, dark pants. We took him out to eat and I bought him a couple of beers. I didn't know he was so unhappy. How did they find him?
He was hanging by his belt in the family house, in his room. His sister found him. She screamed as she ran out.
When's the đám ma?
In 2 days. Do you want to send some money?
I can send 25, you send 25?

II.

Did you hear?
Chị Lanh got into a car accident and is paralyzed from the waist down.
Oh God, no, I didn't know. Who is she again?
She's the daughter of Ba's oldest brother. She took care of you when you were two.
Who's taking care of her?
Her husband is retired, so he's doing most of the work. Her daughter is taking time off from college to help.
Do you want to send some money?
I can't this time because it's tight. Can you send money for me and I'll pay you back later?

III.

Did you hear?
Chị Thu's son just got married. They had a big wedding in Sài Gòn.
Do you mean they went from Đồng Nai to the city to get married? The bride's family must be giàu.
They rented a hall in the city and both families were there. The bride and groom look happy. Chị Thu sent us pictures.
She had to work at a restaurant at nights to pay for the wedding, sell her jewelry. She

74

tried to make him happy, he's the only one she's got left, you know. She chơi hụi but someone took the money.

Are you sending money?

Yeah, how about if I wire 100, and you pay me 50? Even?

Nothing Follows

He's surrounded by walls
          that exhale smoke
                    two fans hover above him,
their blades

sweeping close

He begins and ends the day
          by talking to himself,
                    in 3 different languages

legs crossed, foot tapping
          to a Catholic song,
                    his thumb and finger

      form a hole, like Clinton's

            during a speech

He's talking about

      the past, quá khứ, le passé,
          the recent past, as in mới đây, or le passé récent, or

yesterday, like hôm qua and hier,
                  today, hôm nay, and aujourd'hui,
and even, now, bây giờ, or maintenant

but his words are weeds
          that have followed him

      from north to south, then west

he's raised soldiers for daughters, he hates

      his own kin
          those with his own skin

his stories about

      his children, the ones who did well

               and the ones who did shit

my sisters want him to

      stop talking.   Now.

they say, he remembers

          too much, talks too much

they say, he's become
     lắm chuyện, fussy like

        a woman.

now he lives alone, save

    for a boy
        who answered his call

to share phòng for 100 a week

      in the newspaper *Thằng Mõ*, the Town Crier.

Bones

From the still folds of her aó bà ba, she takes out a wrinkled, dirty bag. She has just come to the US a couple of months ago from Việt Nam. The bag is full of small bones that she has brought, packed them in her handkerchief, and folded neatly in a pocket she has sewn into her shirt.

"The bones of an American soldier, who died near where you were born."

She tells me about my oldest sister in Việt Nam.Tội nghiệp chị lắm. Now that my mother is in the US, she wants to sponsor her eldest daughter over. In pictures, my sister's husband's black hair barely reaches the tops of his sloped shoulders, tense in old shirts we've sent home.

She tells me, two men were in love with her before my father married her but that her family deemed the marriage to my father the most appropriate, and the two men—one a mandarin and the other a poet—were gone.

Now, they hardly speak and live in separate houses. Never left alone. Most days, though, my father wears a blue apron and frets about dinners for friends and neighborhood priests and making things right with god. As for my mother, her hands no longer touch money.

She has been left—twice now—first, when we escaped and she stayed back in Huế, and then second, when she came to cook for a husband who turns away from her rounded back. Wrapping the bones back into her handkerchief, she asks me to buy pig's blood at the local market.

Mary, Joseph, and Jesus

That voice of his crackles
like the cellophane
that covers his smokes.
He's left a message,
the seventh one this week,
he says,

Let me tell you something

At 33, I am no longer his girl.
But he has something to tell me.
He wants me to know his last story,
the one where
he's an honest man.

Let me tell you something

He grips the phone
sitting alone in his apartment
near St. Theresa of Avila Church
on his shelves are his
gold plated trophies
for playing chess
a battalion of medicine
a guitar stoops
in the corner

a three-striped
knitted scarf in the colors
of his flag
is draped onto
the portraits of Mary,
Joseph and Jesus,
they've all surrounded him
in a loving embrace.

Let me tell you something

I hear his voice
but I smell
his apartment first
lemon air and Clorox
every time I visit.
He opens windows
for me, turning on
all three of the ceiling fans
to exile the fumes.

Let me tell you something

His roommate is 18,
he works nightshifts
and helps my father
He's handy
with the computer,
he tells me, and

They live together, an
adopted family
of a man and a boy
under a constantly
moving sun.

One night the boy takes
my father's savings
and hides in his car
for three days.

Let me tell you something

Photograph: Việt Nam, 1995

chị hai, em út,

        people call us.

the ache of ochre blue.

the wetness that stays on our skin,

                the only permanence

    we seem to know.

eyes slouching deep

                    in their sockets

    legs like arms.

lean dogs baring their teeth

           because

        they sense I'm unfamiliar.

i am told by my sisters

                she had to register with the

    new government,

        lined up for rice at dawn

a patch of red earth in Đồng Nai

    in return

              for staying back

on her stomach,

    when she is asleep,

          her fingers are sprawled

like a spider's legs

             and then are deft

    when they lock cabinets doors shutters

        at her home in Việt Nam

to ensure the safety of things

          at the whisper of twilight

Father told me

        that she was his firstborn

curlyhaired like Shirley Temple

                        but that she grew up slow—and slower still

            two photos sit in his album: her wedding and then her firstborn's

wake.

            30 yrs later

i am her sponsor

            petitioning a relative to live in the states looks like this:

                stacks of i-130s affadavits birth certificates taxes money

orders trips

        a watermark on US government letters like a wisp of blood on cool green

she is here visiting while her husband daughter son await her return

           and she cries

                    in the confessional corners of the house

      special powders for her skin

rouge for her winged cheeks

the story of her

              the last one

      to have left

                    is a story of unwarranted theft

Paris by Night

She sees me and clasps my arms and whispers,

have you eaten yet?

She peers into my face as she has done many times before and whispers,

have you eaten yet?

She peers into my face as she has done many times before and whispers,

why don't you have any children?

Má, I have a son. He's two.

She peers into my face as she has done many times before and whispers,

have you eaten yet?

She peers into my face as she has done many times before and whispers,

why don't you have any children?

Má, I have a son. He is two years old.

She peers into my face as she has said done many times before, and whispers,

have you eaten

yet?

Then she laughs, and apropos of nothing, says, I am no longer well.

And I whisper this into one long ear:

Where is your memory?

Can I get it for you?

Where are your stories?

Can I hold them for you?

Where did you go?

Can I follow?

Where the Wild Things Are

I.
Aching for

the girls

we left behind

We bark with throats

coated in smoke.

we've rumpused

and ruckused

on some unnamed island

tattoos

one night in Mexico

coming down

from ecstasy

& shrooms.

II.
Our bodies now

are sheltering sick

handed down

by sisters, brothers,

uncles, aunts

dioxins

from the other country

the pins

holding us

to this here past,

III.

The years stretch out

between us

when

our bodies were

trained

to be

girlboys

goodgirls

prettyyoungthings

and the sex

we once

held between

our legs

furious and

furiouser still

IV.

We still

light up

every now

and then

one finger

of a cigarette

one long drink

of XO

to toast

the girls

we once were

CPSIA information can be obtained
at www.ICGtesting.com
Printed in the USA
LVHW030057010423
743167LV00004B/593